THE ULTIMATE 10

Natural Disasters

EARTHQUAKES

By Anna Prokos

Gareth Stevens
Publishing

Please visit our web site at www.garethstevens.com.
For a free catalog describing Gareth Stevens Publishing's list of high-quality books,
call 1-800-542-2595 (USA) or 1-800-387-3178 (Canada).
Gareth Stevens Publishing's fax: 1-877-542-2596

Library of Congress Cataloging-in-Publication Data
Prokos, Anna.
    Earthquakes / by Anna Prokos.
        p. cm. — (Ultimate 10 : natural disasters)
    Includes bibliographical references and index.
    ISBN-13: 978-0-8368-9151-5 (lib. bdg.)
    ISBN-10: 0-8368-9151-1 (lib. bdg.)
    1. Earthquakes—History—Juvenile literature. I. Title.
QE521.3.P76   2009
551.22—dc22   2008013757

This edition first published in 2009 by
Gareth Stevens Publishing
A Weekly Reader® Company
1 Reader's Digest Rd.
Pleasantville, NY 10570-7000 USA

Senior Managing Editor: Lisa M. Herrington
Senior Editor: Brian Fitzgerald
Creative Director: Lisa Donovan
Senior Designer: Keith Plechaty
Photo Researcher: Charlene Pinckney

Numbers of deaths and injuries from
natural disasters vary from source to
source, particularly for disasters that struck
long ago. The figures included in this book
are based on the best information available
from the most reliable sources.

Picture credits:
Key: t = top, c = center, b = bottom.
Cover, title page: © Nagashima/Pacific Press Service/Alamy; pp. 4–5: © Nik Wheeler/Corbis; p. 7: (t) AFP/Getty Images,
(b) © Corbis; p. 8: Bill Greenblatt/Getty Images; p. 9: AFP/Getty Images; p. 11: © Bettmann/Corbis; p. 12: (t) Peter Bull
Art Studio, (b) U.S. Geological Survey; p. 13: U.S. Geological Survey (both); p. 15: U.S. Geological Survey (both); p. 16:
Wang Jiaowen/AP; p. 17: (t) © Bettmann/Corbis, (b) Science and Society; p. 19: (t) © David Rydevik, (b) © Hellmut
Issels/Newspix; p. 20: (t) Bob Italiano/Weekly Reader, (c, b) DigitalGlobe/Getty Images; p. 21: (t) Dr. Guy Gelfenbaum/
U.S. Geological Survey, (b) Gemunu Amarasinghe/AP; p. 23: (t) © Kimimasa Mayama/Reuters/Corbis, (b) © Mian
Khursheed/Reuters/Corbis; p. 24: (t) BBC News Interactive, (b) Shutterstock; p. 25: NASA (both); p. 27: (t) © Hulton-
Deutsch Collection/Corbis, (b) Brown University Library; p. 29: Toru Yamanaka/AFP/Getty Images; p. 31: (t) © Michael
S. Yamashita/Corbis, (b) Katsumi Kasahara/AP; p. 32: (t) © Nagashima/Pacific Press Service/Alamy (both); p. 33:
(t) © Michael S. Yamashita/Corbis, (b) Kyodo via AP; p. 35: (t) © Bettmann/Corbis, (b) © PoodlesRock/Corbis; p. 36:
© Tom Bean/Corbis; p. 37: (t) U.S. Geological Survey, (c) Corbis; p. 39: (t) © Jim Sugar/Corbis, (b) © Bettmann/Corbis;
p. 40: (t) U.S. Geological Survey, (inset) Chuck Nacke/Time Life Pictures/Getty Images, (b) U.S. Geological Survey;
p. 41: (t) Reed Saxon/AP, (b) U.S. Geological Survey; p. 43: © Owen Franken/Corbis (both); p. 44: (t) © Nik Wheeler/
Corbis, (b) Juan Manuel Villasenor/AP; p. 45: (t) Shutterstock, (b) Yoshikazu Tsuno/AFP/Getty Images; p. 46: (t) Used
with permission of the State Historical Society of Missouri, (c) © Raheb Homavandi/Reuters/Corbis, (b) Cong Feng/
Xinhua/AP.

All maps by Keith Plechaty

Printed in the United States of America

1 2 3 4 5 6 7 8 9 10 09 08

Table of Contents

Words in the glossary appear in **bold** type
the first time they are used in the text.

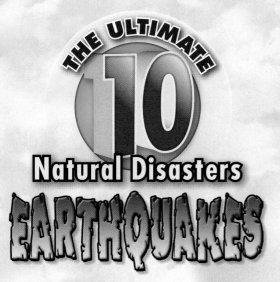

THE ULTIMATE 10
Natural Disasters
EARTHQUAKES

Welcome to The Ultimate 10! This exciting series explores Earth's most powerful and unforgettable natural disasters.

In this book, you'll get a groundbreaking look at earthquakes: how and why they happen, what damage they cause, and what to do if "the big one" hits!

Mexico City, 1985

Nothing shakes up our planet quite the way an earthquake does. Earthquakes are sudden movements in Earth's **crust**, or rocky outer layer. They are caused by a release of great pressure inside our planet.

A strong earthquake usually causes violent shaking. Earthquakes can shake the ground from left to right or up and down. Earthquakes can even form—or move—mountains! Earth experiences about 8,000 quakes every day. Most are too small to be felt. The rare, powerful earthquakes are the ones that people don't forget.

What's Shaking?

Here's a look at 10 earthquakes that have rocked our world.

#1 Great Chile Earthquake, 1960

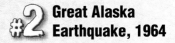
#2 Great Alaska Earthquake, 1964

#3 Tangshan Earthquake, 1976

#4 Indian Ocean Earthquake, 2004

#5 Great Pakistan Earthquake, 2005

#6 Great Kanto Earthquake, 1923

#7 Kobe Earthquake, 1995

#8 San Francisco Earthquake, 1906

#9 Loma Prieta Earthquake, 1989

#10 Mexico City Earthquake, 1985

Great Chile Earthquake
Strongest Recorded Quake in History

On the morning of May 22, 1960, strong tremors stunned the people of Valdivia, Chile. A powerful earthquake struck 180 feet (55 meters) below the sea, nearly 100 miles (160 kilometers) out into the Pacific Ocean. The largest earthquake ever recorded sent severe shocks through the ground. Within minutes, Valdivia and other towns along Chile's coast were in ruins.

FAST FACTS

Great Chile Earthquake

Date: May 22, 1960

Location: Near Valdivia, Chile

Magnitude: 9.5

Impact: 1,655 killed, 3,000 injured, 2,000,000 homeless

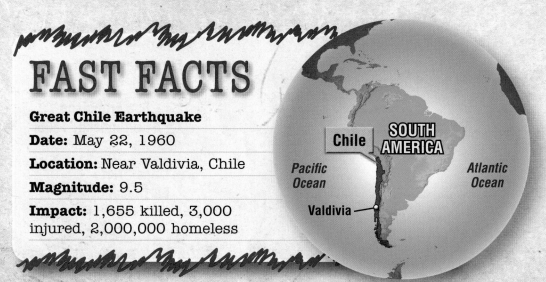

SOUTH AMERICA

Chile

Pacific Ocean

Atlantic Ocean

Valdivia

The powerful earthquake caused many homes near the coast of Chile to crumble to pieces.

Walls of Water

Less than 15 minutes after the tremors, a **tsunami**, or massive ocean wave, smacked the coast of Chile. The wall of water reached 80 feet (24 m) high! Boats were totally wiped out—along with streets and buildings. Everything was destroyed in Chile's coastal towns.

The Terror Spreads

The damage didn't end there. Within 15 hours, tsunamis hit Hilo, Hawaii— about 6,600 miles (10,600 km) away! The 30-foot (9-m) waves killed 61 people.

There was more to come. Seven hours later, tsunamis hit the coast of Japan. The 18-foot (5.5-m) waves caused 200 deaths. In all, the quake and tsunamis killed 1,655 people worldwide.

The tsunami tore apart houses in Hilo, Hawaii.

Measuring Up

Scientists measure the strength of an earthquake with **seismographs**. These instruments measure how much the ground shakes. The Great Chile Earthquake was the first in history to be accurately measured by seismographs.

Magnitude

The best way to measure a quake is to figure out its **magnitude**. Magnitude is a measure of the energy released by an earthquake. Scientists estimate magnitude by reading seismographs.

Magnitude is measured on a scale of 1 to 10. The strongest quakes are very rare. Each year, about one quake with a magnitude of 8.0 or greater hits somewhere in the world. The Great Chile Earthquake measured 9.5—the highest magnitude ever recorded.

Strongest shaking

The lines on a seismograph show how much the ground shakes during an earthquake. The wider the lines, the stronger the shaking. This reading is from a very strong quake.

Biggest Quakes

Take a look at the five largest earthquakes since 1900.

Location	Date	Magnitude
1. Near coast of Chile	May 22, 1960	9.5
2. Near Anchorage, Alaska	March 28, 1964	9.2
3. Indian Ocean	December 26, 2004	9.1
4. Kamchatka, Russia	November 4, 1952	9.0
5. Near coast of Ecuador	January 31, 1906	8.8

Source: U.S. Geological Survey

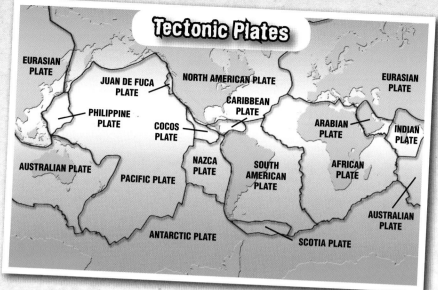

Tectonic Plates

EURASIAN PLATE
JUAN DE FUCA PLATE
NORTH AMERICAN PLATE
EURASIAN PLATE
PHILIPPINE PLATE
CARIBBEAN PLATE
ARABIAN PLATE
INDIAN PLATE
COCOS PLATE
AUSTRALIAN PLATE
NAZCA PLATE
SOUTH AMERICAN PLATE
AFRICAN PLATE
PACIFIC PLATE
AUSTRALIAN PLATE
ANTARCTIC PLATE
SCOTIA PLATE

How Quakes Happen

Earth's crust is made up of huge slabs of rock called **tectonic plates**. The plates may slowly move apart from each other. They also may slip by each other or crash into one another. Plates usually move about as fast as your fingernails grow. Sometimes plates move suddenly. This movement causes earthquakes.

Faults, or breaks in Earth's crust, appear along plate edges. Many earthquakes happen near faults. During the Chile quake, part of the Nazca Plate about the size of California slid 50 feet (15 m) beneath South America. The extreme movement pushed the land upward and dropped the coast of Chile about 10 feet (3 m).

In Valdivia, the ground movement split a street down the middle.

Did You Know?

The Great Chile Earthquake was so strong that it triggered a volcanic eruption. The Cordón Caulle sent steam and ash into the air two days after the quake. Lava continued to flow out of the volcano for more than a month.

#2
Great Alaska Earthquake
Largest Quake in the United States

Alaska was rocked by the strongest earthquake in U.S. history on March 28, 1964. People in Anchorage, the state's biggest city, heard a rumbling sound shortly after 5:30 p.m. The 9.2 magnitude quake shook the ground violently for four minutes. Thirty minutes after the tremors, a giant tsunami swept across the Pacific Ocean.

FAST FACTS

Great Alaska Earthquake

Date: March 28, 1964

Location: Near Anchorage, AK

Magnitude: 9.2

Impact: 128 killed

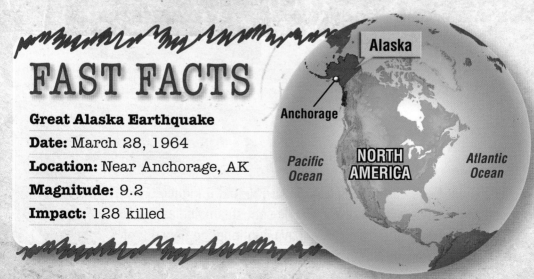

Alaska

Anchorage

Pacific Ocean

NORTH AMERICA

Atlantic Ocean

A Big Drop
The earthquake cracked, tore, and split roads in half. Fourth Avenue in downtown Anchorage dropped 20 feet (6 m) below its normal level.

Shaken Up

The strong motions caused some parts of the ground to rise by more than 30 feet (9 m)! In one coastal town, part of the waterfront slid into the bay.

The quake wasn't just the largest to hit the United States. It was also the second-largest recorded quake in history. Alaska is one of the least-populated states. If more people had lived in the area, the death toll of 128 would have been much higher.

Eyewitness

" The noise of the earth's rumbling and the crashing of dishes alerted me instantly that something was terribly [wrong]. Seconds after the rumbling and violent shaking began, Mother screamed ... 'Get out! Get outside!' " — Georgiana Llaneza, Anchorage resident

Starting Point

The **focus** is the point where an earthquake begins. It can be close to Earth's surface or hundreds of miles deep in the ground. A quake close to the surface causes the most violent tremors—and plenty of damage. The focus of the Alaska quake was only 14 miles (22.5 km) below the surface. That explains why the shaking was so extreme.

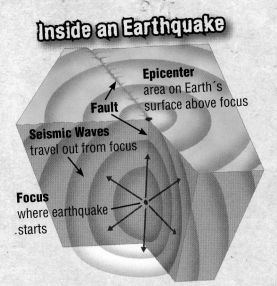

Inside an Earthquake

Epicenter area on Earth's surface above focus

Fault

Seismic Waves travel out from focus

Focus where earthquake starts

The **epicenter** is the point on the surface directly above the focus. **Seismic waves** travel out from the epicenter. The waves move in circles, like the ripples you see when you throw a stone into a puddle. Scientists locate the epicenter by studying the direction of the seismic waves. Areas close to the epicenter get hit the hardest.

Collapsed six-story building

Cracked ground

Anchorage was only 75 miles (121 km) from the epicenter. The city had severe damage to prove it.

Triggering Disaster

Earthquakes can set off landslides, causing hills and mountainsides to fall. Landslides caused much of the damage in Anchorage.

This school in Anchorage was ripped in half by a landslide.

A tsunami whipped through Kodiak Island, Alaska. The huge wave washed out the entire waterfront.

Spreading Out

This quake affected many parts of the United States. A tsunami that started in Alaska killed 11 people in Crescent City, California. In Texas and Florida, the ground rippled up 2 to 4 inches (5 to 10 centimeters).

Did You Know?

Alaska is the most earthquake-prone state. The area has a magnitude 7 quake almost every year. Experts say a quake of magnitude 8 or higher will probably strike Alaska every 14 years.

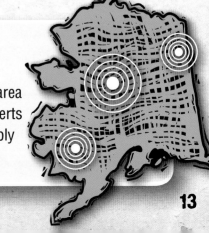

#3
Tangshan Earthquake
Deadliest Earthquake in Modern History

It took only 16 seconds for an earthquake to level the entire city of Tangshan, China. The quake struck as most of the 1.6 million residents slept on July 27, 1976. Intense shaking demolished 85 percent of the city's buildings. Highways and roads collapsed. People were trapped in the rubble for days.

FAST FACTS

Tangshan Earthquake
Date: July 27, 1976
Location: Near Tangshan, China
Magnitude: 7.5
Impact: 255,000 killed

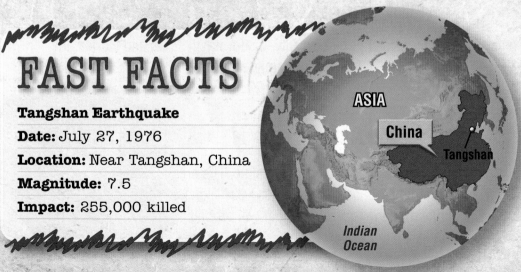

ASIA

China

Tangshan

Indian Ocean

Eyewitness

" It was horrible. We were lost. Like an ocean, an ocean, everything moving. "
— Maurice Monge, a French tourist visiting Tangshan

Before the quake struck, this pile of rocks was a four-story bank.

Reduced to Rubble

When the shaking stopped, people rushed out of their homes to see a flattened city. Screams echoed from beneath piles of rubble.

As survivors waited to be rescued, an **aftershock**, or smaller quake, hit. Usually, shocks that follow the main quake are much less intense. But this 7.1 magnitude shock caused more damage. People waiting for help were killed. Water lines broke, and electricity shut down.

Roads into the city were blocked with wreckage. Survivors were left without food or clean drinking water. The official death toll reached 255,000. Some sources claim that as many as 650,000 people died.

Collapsed bridge

A collapsed bridge made it hard for help to reach Tangshan.

Tracking Quakes

China has the oldest earthquake records in the world. As far back as 780 B.C., the Chinese kept records of earthquakes and other natural disasters. The ancient records show that the country has been struck by many deadly quakes throughout history.

On May 12, 2008, a 7.9 earthquake rocked southern China. It was China's worst earthquake since the 1976 Tangshan quake.

Why does China get hit so hard? The country is at the center of one of the most active seismic areas in the world. It is also the most populated country in the world. Thousands of people can be killed when a quake strikes.

Deadliest Quakes in History

China has been hit with many of the deadliest quakes of all time.

Location	Date	Deaths
1. Shaanxi, China	January 23, 1556	830,000
2. Tangshan, China	July 27, 1976	255,000
3. Aleppo, Syria	August 9, 1138	230,000
4. Indian Ocean	December 26, 2004	227,898
5. Damghan, Iran	December 22, 856	200,000
6. Ningxia, China	December 16, 1920	200,000
7. Ardabil, Iran	March 23, 893	150,000
8. Kanto, Japan	September 1, 1923	142,800
9. Ashgabat, Turkmenistan	October 5, 1948	110,000
10. Chihli, China	September 27, 1290	100,000

Source: U.S. Geological Survey

Predicting Quakes

The Chinese tried to predict earthquakes by studying patterns in nature. Strange animal behavior, they believed, signaled that a quake was on its way.

In February 1975, several snakes came out of hibernation early. The reptiles froze on the winter ground. Experts warned that a big quake was coming. The warning saved thousands of lives when a 7.3 magnitude quake struck two months later. No such warning came before the Tangshan quake, however.

Did You Know?

The Chinese invented the first device for measuring earthquakes nearly 2,000 years ago. The jar was decorated with dragons and frogs. When the jar shook, a ball rolled from a dragon's mouth into a frog's mouth. This showed the direction of the shaking. One legend says that the instrument detected a quake 400 miles (644 km) away.

Indian Ocean Earthquake
Biggest Quake of the 21st Century

On December 26, 2004, serious trouble was brewing deep in the Indian Ocean. The Indian Plate shifted sideways under the Eurasian Plate for 10 minutes. The result was a massive 9.1 magnitude quake. Instantly, killer 50-foot (15-m) tsunamis rushed to the coasts along the Indian Ocean. More than 225,000 people in 11 countries were killed.

FAST FACTS

Indian Ocean Earthquake

Date: December 26, 2004

Location: Off coast of Indonesia

Magnitude: 9.1

Impact: 227,898 killed

As the wall of water hit Ao Nang, Thailand, people ran to escape. Luckily, everyone in this photo survived the killer tsunami.

Killer Wave

The coast of the Indian Ocean is lined with vacation spots. Resorts dot the beaches. On December 26, people saw a big, black wave approaching—fast.

The first tsunami rushed ashore with amazing speed. It swept up everything along with it. Minutes later, the wave retreated into the sea with extreme force. Like a bathtub drain, it sucked everything

Powerful waves swept through a resort in Phuket, Thailand.

back into the ocean. Two more waves came, each more powerful and deadly than the next.

How a Tsunami Forms

A tsunami is triggered by sudden changes to the ocean floor. This massive quake caused the seafloor to shift up 40 feet (12 m) in some places! The shake-up of the seafloor sent a wall of water toward the coast. The massive wave traveled at 300 miles (483 km) per hour. The tsunami hit Indonesia about 75 minutes after the quake.

Earthquake epicenter

A tsunami gets bigger and bigger as it moves toward the shore.

BEFORE

Before and After
Banda Aceh, Indonesia, was the closest city to the quake's epicenter. The satellite photo on top shows the area months before the disaster. The bottom photo shows the area wiped out by the tsunami.

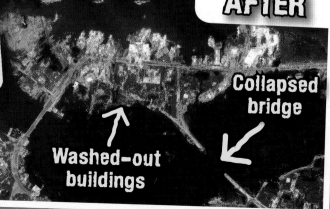
AFTER

Collapsed bridge

Washed-out buildings

Eyewitness

❝ Buildings are crushed, flattened, and splintered. Cars and buses look as if they've been picked up and tossed. You can smell death in the air. ❞
—Tom Costanza, cameraman who helped with relief efforts in Banda Aceh

The massive tsunami wiped out nearly everything in Banda Aceh. Only a handful of buildings withstood the powerful waves.

Warning Signs

Thousands of lives might have been saved if people had been warned about the tsunami. Today, countries around the Indian Ocean have a warning system in place. Sensors in the Indian Ocean detect seafloor movement. Seismograph stations on land monitor ground movements. The Indian Ocean Tsunami Warning System should help save people the next time a tsunami strikes.

Did You Know?

After the tsunami, a two-month-old baby was found on a beach in Sri Lanka. The wave had swept him from his mother's arms. Somehow the miracle baby survived. He was nicknamed "Baby 81" because he was the 81st victim brought to the local hospital. More than six weeks after the disaster, he was returned to his parents.

#5

Great Pakistan Earthquake
Quake With the Most Challenging Relief Efforts

On the morning of October 8, 2005, a major earthquake struck Kashmir, Pakistan. Kids were just starting their school day. The severe shaking left many schools and other buildings in ruins. This was the strongest quake in the area since 1900. The rescue and relief effort would be a major challenge.

FAST FACTS

Great Pakistan Earthquake

Date: October 8, 2005

Location: Kashmir, Pakistan

Magnitude: 7.6

Impact: 86,000 killed, 69,000 injured, 4 million homeless

ASIA

Pakistan

Indian Ocean

No Relief

The quake caused major landslides that blocked roads for weeks. Heavy snowfall and cold winter weather set in. The weather stopped helicopters and trucks from delivering food, water, and supplies. People were in danger of freezing or starving to death.

Landslides blocked many mountain roads. Mules carried food and supplies to survivors.

The earthquake reduced roads and buildings to rubble. Rescue workers gathered to begin difficult rescue operations.

Eyewitness

❝ Rocks were rolling down the mountain towards us ... there was an enormous cloak of dust. There was a thick fog—it was as if the mountain was boiling. ❞

—Ahsan Haque, a hiker who was close to the epicenter

Crash Course

The Great Pakistan Earthquake occurred where the Indian and Eurasian plates meet. The Himalaya Mountains were formed as the plates began colliding about 70 million years ago. As the plates continue to push together, Earth's tallest mountains keep getting taller. Each year, the Himalayas rise about two-tenths of an inch.

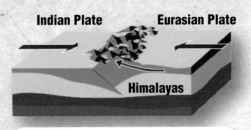

The colliding plates force rock layers upward. As a result, the Himalayas keep getting taller.

Mount Everest in the Himalayas is the tallest mountain on Earth. The constant collision of the Indian and Eurasian plates makes Everest taller each year.

Seen From Space

Satellite images tell us a lot about Earth after a quake. Satellite images can help rescuers see which areas were badly damaged. This helps them plan the best ways to get relief to those areas.

BEFORE

Neelum River

AFTER

Water turned brown

Landslide

Before and After

These images show a landslide that sent part of a mountain into the Neelum River in Pakistan. Before the quake, the river was clearly visible—and blue. After, rubble from landslides turned the river brown. The white part of the mountain is the rock and soil that slid down during the quake.

Did You Know?

The Great Pakistan Earthquake set off an even greater relief effort. Thousands of volunteers helped rebuild homes, roads, hospitals, and schools. One government group sent 18,000 tents and 505,000 blankets. It also sent more than 31,500 mattresses, almost 50,000 sleeping bags, and several tons of medical supplies.

25

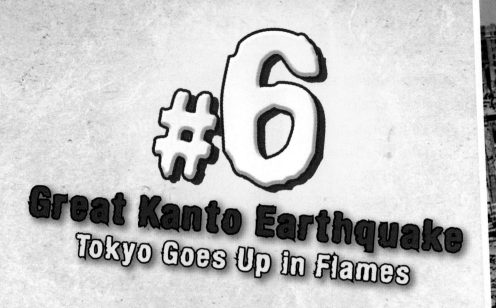

#6
Great Kanto Earthquake
Tokyo Goes Up in Flames

Just as restaurants in Tokyo, Japan, fired up their gas stoves to prepare lunch, the ground started shaking. It swayed for four minutes. Extreme destruction swept through Japan's capital city. Gas lines in homes and restaurants burst. Fires raged everywhere. Witnesses said the city looked like a war zone.

FAST FACTS

Great Kanto Earthquake

Date: September 1, 1923

Location: Near Tokyo, Japan

Magnitude: 7.9

Impact: 142,800 killed

ASIA

Japan

Tokyo

Pacific Ocean

Many buildings in Tokyo were burned out. Others were totally flattened.

Fire's Fury

During the quake, hot coals used for cooking were scattered around homes. Fires began to rage in nearly every neighborhood. Water mains burst, so firefighters couldn't put out the rising flames. Fires swallowed up strong, wooden homes that had survived the quake.

In Yokohama, Japan, smoke filled the sky as fires broke out after the quake.

Big Wave

The floor of Tokyo Bay shifted during the quake. That movement caused a tsunami with waves as high as 40 feet (12 m). The wave struck the coastal town of Atami, killing 60 people.

The Ring of Fire

Japan is part of the Ring of Fire. This horseshoe-shaped area runs along the edge of the Pacific Ocean. The Ring of Fire is about 25,000 miles (40,234 km) long. It follows the border of major tectonic plates. It is lined with many major volcanoes and is the site of serious seismic activity. About 90 percent of the world's earthquakes occur in the area.

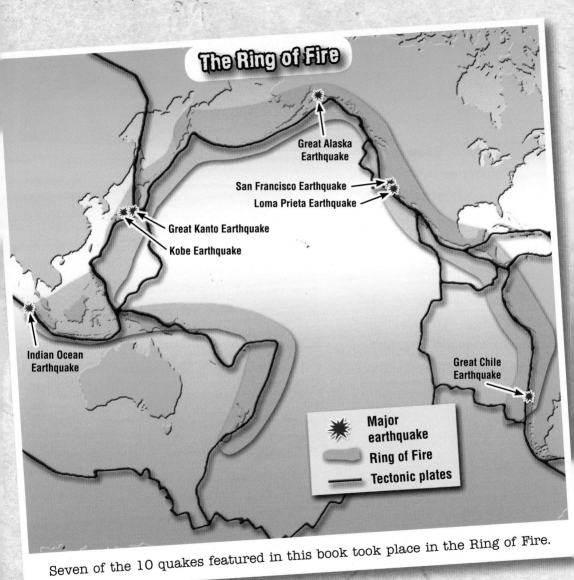

Seven of the 10 quakes featured in this book took place in the Ring of Fire.

Japanese children wear special fire-resistant hoods during an earthquake drill.

Disaster Prevention

After the quake, preventing future disasters became a main concern for Japanese officials. That's why they named September 1 as Disaster Prevention Day. People learn what to do in case an earthquake or other disaster strikes.

September 1 is often the first day of school for students in Japan. On that day, children follow disaster prevention drills. They learn to duck and take cover under desks. They practice escape routes. Then teachers talk to them about the Great Kanto Earthquake.

Did You Know?

QUAKE SINKS TOKYO?

Gathering facts about the quake was tough. Most reporters couldn't get to the area. Many papers reported rumors as truth. Some newspaper articles claimed that Tokyo had been completely wiped out. One paper declared that the entire area had sunk into the sea!

#7
Kobe Earthquake
Costliest Quake in History

Past earthquakes had taught the Japanese to be prepared. Still, people were taken by surprise when an earthquake struck Kobe, Japan, on January 16, 1995. The ground shook beneath the city for 20 terrifying seconds. Buildings trembled, apartments pancaked, and houses collapsed. Gas lines broke and chemicals burned. Within minutes, more than 300 fires lit up the morning sky.

FAST FACTS

Kobe Earthquake

Date: January 16, 1995

Location: Near Kobe, Japan

Magnitude: 6.8

Impact: 5,502 killed

ASIA

Japan

Kobe

Pacific Ocean

Strong tremors caused buildings and other structures to sway. Railroad tracks twisted and leaned over a train station in Kobe.

Chaos in the City

The quake's epicenter was just 20 miles (32 km) away from Kobe. It was the closest a big quake had ever struck to a major city.

Kobe was considered a low-risk area for earthquakes. Building codes weren't as strict as in other parts of Japan. Most homes and buildings couldn't stand up to the severe shaking. The result was the costliest quake ever. The city suffered about $100 billion in damages.

Volunteers rescued people from collapsed and burning buildings.

The quake and fires left people in Kobe without water and electricity. One million households had no electricity for an entire week. Repair crews needed more than three months to get water back to 1.3 million homes.

Falling From Above

More than 103,500 buildings were destroyed. Some homes had heavy tiles on the roof. The tiles were meant to withstand severe storms called typhoons. The weight of the tiles made the homes buckle in the quake.

Smashed tile roof

Lost Highway

The Hanshin Expressway is a major roadway in Kobe. During the quake, some columns that held up the highway crumbled. Huge sections of the highway toppled.

Flipped trucks

Turning to Mush

A lot of the ground in Kobe turned to jelly in the quake. This is called **liquefaction**, which happens when water-filled soil acts like a liquid. The soil couldn't support weight. Buildings and roads cracked and collapsed.

Collapsed road

The quake caused roads along the Kobe waterfront to crumble. The roads, and the cars on them, plunged into the water.

Smart Building

Quakeproof building materials are now a must in Kobe. Rubber blocks on bridges absorb shocks and keep the structures from falling. Concrete highway columns are now stronger and wider to hold up roads. New structures can withstand strong tremors. Homes are spaced farther apart so they cannot fall like dominoes. These safety measures will save lives if another quake hits.

Did You Know?

An annual light festival is held in memory of the victims of the Kobe Earthquake. Nearly 5 million people visit the festival each December.

33

#8
1906 San Francisco Earthquake
A Quake That Changed a City

A loud rumble shook the quiet morning in San Francisco, California, on April 18, 1906. People were rattled out of bed and thrown to the floor. One minute of powerful shaking changed the city forever. Smoke and dust covered the streets. People tried to escape without getting crushed or burned.

FAST FACTS

1906 San Francisco Earthquake

Date: April 18, 1906

Location: Near San Francisco, CA

Magnitude: 7.8 (estimated)

Impact: more than 3,000 killed

California

San Francisco

NORTH AMERICA

Atlantic Ocean

Pacific Ocean

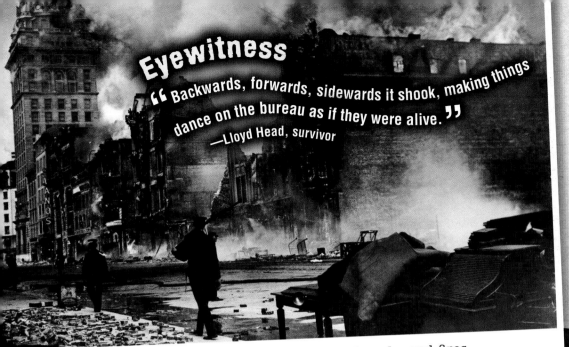

Eyewitness

" Backwards, forwards, sidewards it shook, making things dance on the bureau as if they were alive. "
—Lloyd Head, survivor

Chaos broke out in San Francisco after the earthquake and fires. Army troops patrolled the streets to try to keep order.

Shaken and Stirred

People still in their pajamas rushed to the streets. Once outside, they could see the devastation. Brick chimneys had smashed to pieces. Tops of buildings had been shaken off. Many streets split in two.

The Big Burn

For three days, flames burned through sections of the city. The water mains had been damaged. Firefighters couldn't use water to put out the flames. Instead, they blasted buildings with dynamite to keep fires from spreading. The blasts created more fires, and the inferno kept blazing.

Some survivors said they were nearly swallowed up as the streets cracked open.

Famous Fault

San Francisco sits very close to the San Andreas Fault. The famous fault lies between the Pacific and North American plates. It stretches for almost 800 miles (1,290 km) and reaches 10 miles (16 km) deep into the ground.

During the 1906 quake, both sides of the fault slipped past each other horizontally. About 300 miles (483 km) of the San Andreas Fault split during the quake. It was the longest rupture of a fault in the United States.

About 10,000 quakes occur along the San Andreas Fault each year. Luckily, most are too minor to be felt.

San Andreas Fault

California

San Francisco

Los Angeles

The major shaking threw this train off its tracks.

City Under Siege

The earthquake and the fires created total chaos in San Francisco. To keep people from looting, the mayor declared a new rule. Anyone caught stealing or making trouble would be shot on the spot.

About 4,000 Army soldiers were sent to help out after the quake. They guarded the U.S. Mint, post office, and jails. The Army also helped thousands of people receive food and housing. The soldiers helped set up tents and medical stations.

Did You Know?

The quake in San Francisco shook seismographs on the other side of the world. Tremors were detected by a seismograph in Gottingen, Germany—more than 5,600 miles (9,000 km) away.

#9

Loma Prieta Earthquake
First Televised Earthquake

The 1906 earthquake wasn't the last disaster to rock northern California. As fans shuffled into Candlestick Park to watch the 1989 World Series, a 7.1 magnitude quake struck the area. People tuning in to watch the game were shocked. It was the first time an earthquake was shown live on television.

FAST FACTS

Loma Prieta Earthquake
Date: October 17, 1989
Location: Near San Francisco, CA
Magnitude: 7.1
Impact: 63 killed

California

San Francisco

NORTH AMERICA

Atlantic Ocean

Pacific Ocean

Fallen Freeway

People were killed when major freeways collapsed because of the quake. The Cypress Viaduct is a double-deck freeway that swayed and rippled during the quake. The top part of the viaduct collapsed onto the lower level, killing 42 people.

Spreading Terror

The city of Santa Cruz was 10 miles (16 km) from the epicenter. It was also the first to be torn apart. The damage continued as the tremors moved toward San Francisco. In all, 63 people died and 28,000 buildings were damaged.

Eyewitness

" Imagine Candlestick Park completely coming apart and going back together... Then to look out to the field and just see it roll as if it were an ocean. **"**

—Army Staff Sergeant David Longdon

Scared players and fans rushed onto the field at Candlestick Park.

Broken Bridge

Part of the San Francisco-Oakland Bay Bridge collapsed. A car drove off the edge of the gap and crashed to the lower deck. The driver was killed.

When part of the San Francisco-Oakland Bay Bridge collapsed, two cars were wedged between the decks of the bridge.

Shake, Rattle, and Roll

San Francisco's Marina District suffered severe damage. A total of 35 buildings were completely demolished. Land in the Marina District was created when a lagoon was filled with sand and rubble from the 1906 quake. The loose ground became like quicksand. Buildings constructed on the landfill collapsed.

In San Francisco's Marina District, buildings crumbled to matchsticks when the unstable ground turned to liquid.

Better Prepared

The San Francisco downtown area was wiped out in 1906. The rebuilt area was largely undamaged by the 1989 quake. After the 1906 quake, builders learned an important lesson. They used materials that can bend and stretch without breaking. Many of the city's buildings are now strong enough to withstand a major earthquake.

More Major Quakes?

A year after the quake, scientists studied the chances of a large earthquake hitting near San Francisco again. They estimate that a 6.7 or higher quake will likely hit the area by 2030.

Scientists measure soil layers in the San Andreas Fault. This helps them learn about historical quakes that have hit the area.

Did You Know?

The quake was named after Loma Prieta Peak in the Santa Cruz Mountains. The peak is close to where the jolts began.

#10
Mexico City Earthquake
Quake in a Sinking City

On September 19, 1985, three minutes of intense tremors turned Mexico City into a zone of extreme destruction. The 8.0 magnitude quake turned high-rises into rubble. The ground around the city had sunk several inches. Buildings crumbled. Thirty-six hours after the quake, a 7.5 magnitude aftershock hit the area.

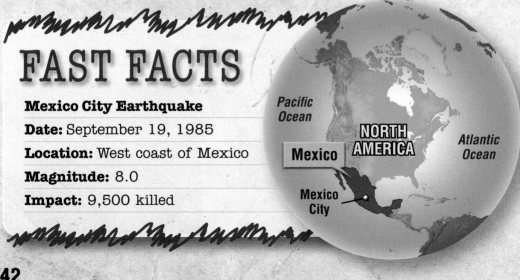

FAST FACTS

Mexico City Earthquake

Date: September 19, 1985

Location: West coast of Mexico

Magnitude: 8.0

Impact: 9,500 killed

Pacific Ocean

NORTH AMERICA

Atlantic Ocean

Mexico

Mexico City

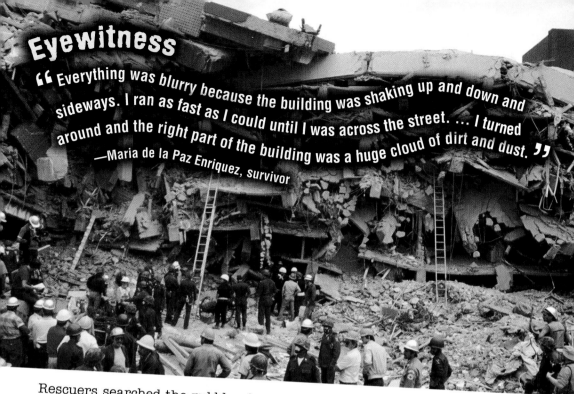

Rescuers searched the rubble of a fallen building for survivors.

To the Rescue

Mexico City's population was 18 million at the time. That's about twice the number of people living in New York City today. Many victims were children. Amazing rescue efforts helped save 58 babies trapped inside a fallen hospital.

Rescuers used dogs to search for survivors. The dogs' keen sense of smell helped them sniff out people trapped in the rubble.

Ground Rules

The quake's focus was about 186 miles (300 km) away from Mexico City. Why was the city hit so hard? Mexico City sits on an ancient lake that has been drained. The lake's silt and sand are now the city's foundation. Liquefaction turned the ground to jelly, causing buildings to sink and collapse.

Rock Solid

Structures built on **bedrock**, the hardest ground material, have the least movement during a quake. Land that's mostly sand and gravel feels slightly stronger tremors. Soft mud causes the most jolting movement. Structures built on soft mud will completely collapse during a major quake.

Toppled buildings crushed cars parked on the streets of Mexico City.

Did You Know?

Opera singer Placido Domingo rushed to Mexico City to rescue earthquake survivors. Four of his relatives died in the tragedy. Shortly after, he held concerts and raised more than $2 million to help quake victims.

Be Prepared!

Experts say parts of Mexico, California, and other areas around the world could get hit with "the big one." Here's how to stay safe.

Before a Quake

- ☑ Make your home safe. Keep heavy items away from your bed. Secure furniture to the wall. Keep cabinets and drawers latched so items don't slide out.

- ☑ Make a survival kit. Pack enough water and food for three days for every person and pet in your family. Pack warm clothes and sturdy shoes. Include flashlights, batteries, and a fire extinguisher.

- ☑ Create an earthquake plan. State where to go for help. Identify someone to check in with if you become separated from your family.

During a Quake

- ☑ Drop, cover, and hold your head and neck. Stay inside—but away from windows—until the shaking stops.

- ☑ Go to the nearest exit when the ground stops moving.

After the Quake

- ☑ Check yourself and others for injuries.

- ☑ Listen to the radio for instructions.

- ☑ If you feel aftershocks, drop, cover, and hold.

Students in Tokyo take part in an earthquake drill.

Source: American Red Cross

Honorable Mentions

New Madrid Earthquake
December 16, 1811, and January 23, 1812

Sometimes earthquakes occur far from plate boundaries. Three such quakes rattled New Madrid, Missouri, during the winter of 1811–1812. Each had a magnitude of 8 or higher. The violent tremors reshaped the land. Some lakes were permanently drained. Forests were wiped out. New lakes were formed by the quakes and thousands of aftershocks.

Southeastern Iran Earthquake
December 26, 2003

Exactly one year before the Indian Ocean earthquake, a 6.6 magnitude quake rippled through southeastern Iran. More than 31,000 people died. The area suffered more than $30 million in damages. Scientists say it was the largest—and deadliest—quake to hit the area in more than two centuries.

Great Sichuan Earthquake
May 12, 2008

A huge 7.9 quake killed more than 71,000 people in southern China on May 12, 2008. Eighty percent of the buildings in Sichuan province collapsed. The quake was followed by hundreds of powerful aftershocks. More than 5 million people were left homeless.

Glossary

aftershock: a smaller quake that follows the largest shock of an earthquake. Aftershocks can continue over a period of hours, weeks, months, or years.

bedrock: hard, solid rock beneath soil

crust: the outermost layer of Earth

epicenter: the point on Earth's surface that's directly above where an earthquake begins underground

fault: a fracture, or break, that usually forms near plate boundaries

focus: the point within Earth where an earthquake begins

liquefaction: the changing of soil into a fluidlike substance during an earthquake

magnitude: a number that describes the strength of an earthquake. It is based on the maximum motion recorded by a seismograph.

seismic waves: energy that ripples out from an earthquake

seismograph: an instrument used to detect and record earthquakes

tectonic plates: huge pieces of Earth's crust that move and slide near one another

tsunami: a sea wave that is created when the seafloor moves because of large earthquakes, landslides, or erupting volcanoes

For More Information

Books

Cooke, Tim. *1906 San Francisco Earthquake* (Disasters series). Pleasantville, N.Y.: Gareth Stevens, 2005.

Fradin, J., and D. Fradin. *Witness to Disaster: Earthquakes.* Washington, D.C.: National Geographic Society, 2008.

Rubin, Ken. *Volcanoes & Earthquakes* (Insiders). New York: Simon & Schuster Children's Publishing, 2007.

Simon, Seymour. *Earthquakes.* New York: Harper Collins, 2006.

Van Rose, Susanna. *Volcanoes and Earthquakes* (DK Eyewitness Books). New York: Dorling-Kindersley, 2004.

Web Sites

United States Geological Survey Earthquake Hazards Program: earthquake.usgs.gov

Trigger a quake: www.nationalgeographic.com/forcesofnature/interactive/index.html?section=e

Watch a quake simulator in action: www.sciencedaily.com/videos/2007/0112-earthquake_test_building_better_homes.htm

Publisher's note to educators and parents: Our editors have carefully reviewed these web sites to ensure that they are suitable for children. Many web sites change frequently, however, and we cannot guarantee that a site's future contents will continue to meet our high standards of quality and educational value. Be advised that children should be closely supervised whenever they access the Internet.

Index

About the Author

Anna Prokos likes to keep her feet on stable ground! She once experienced a mild earthquake while on vacation in Greece—and it was pretty jolting. Prokos lives with her husband and two sons in New Jersey, where she writes a lot of science, history, and reading books for kids.